This book belongs to:

**For those who dare to be different,
may your uniqueness shine bright.**

Higgzfield Tales
Published in Canada
Written by: Marissa J. Salvas
Illustrated by: Marina Aguirre
Text and illustrations copyright © 2021 Higgzfield Ltd.

ISBN 978-1-7388583-2-3 (hardcover)
ISBN 978-1-7388583-3-0 (paperback)
ISBN 978-1-7388583-4-7 (digital)

First Edition
Winston Discovers His Roots

All rights reserved. No part of this book may be
reproduced or used in any manner without written
permission of the copyright owner. For more
information: hello@higgzfield.com.

For more insights and activities, visit us at
www.higgzfield.com.

HiGGZ
FiELD™

HiGGZFiELD™

Winston Discovers His Roots

by Marissa J. Salvas

Illustrated by Marina Aguirre

Not too far away,
warmed by the sun,
kissed by the wind,
positioned by the stars,
mooned by the moon,
hugged by a great forest,
the creatures frolicked
in a place called Higgzfield.

WELCOME
TO
HIGGZFIELD

"Good morning, Winston," said Miss Higgz.

Winston woke up with cool water tickling his toes, the fresh breeze blowing through his hair, and the warmth of the sun on his back. He stretched and wiggled his toes.

As Winston looked around at the creatures in the meadow, he began to wonder who he was.

"Am I a snail like you, Shirley?" asked Winston.

"Not so fast, Winston. Time will tell." Shirley chuckled.

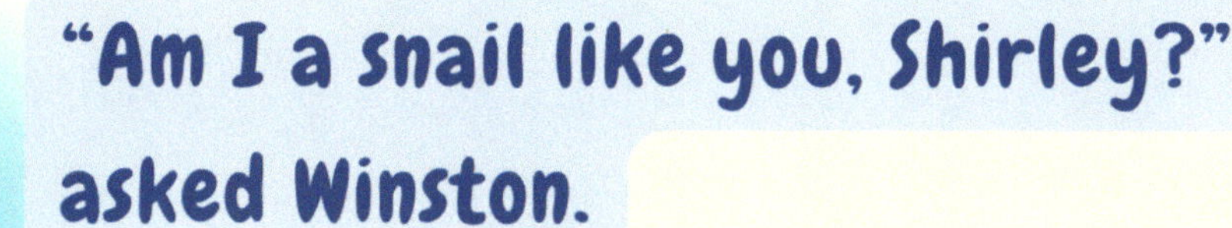

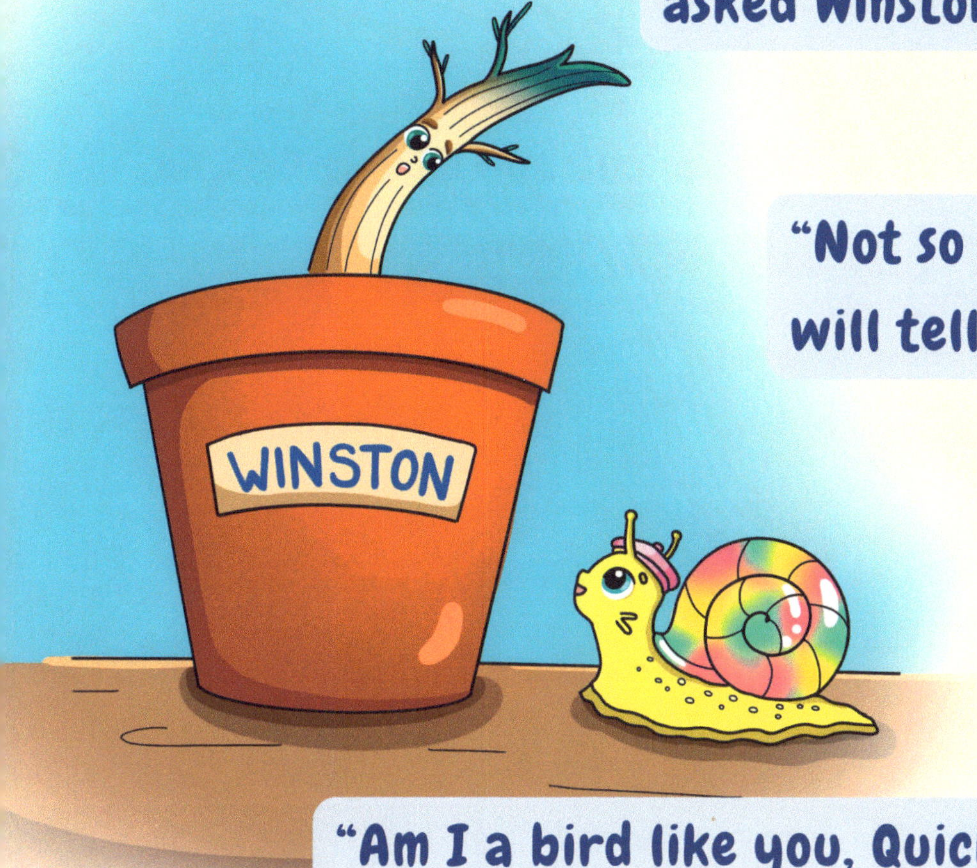

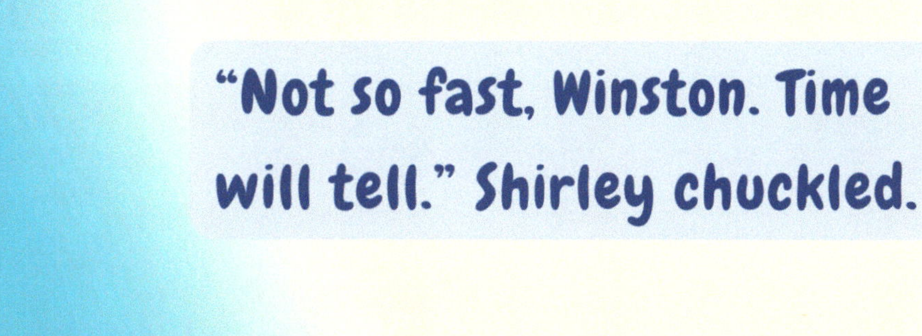

"Am I a bird like you, Quiche?" asked Winston.

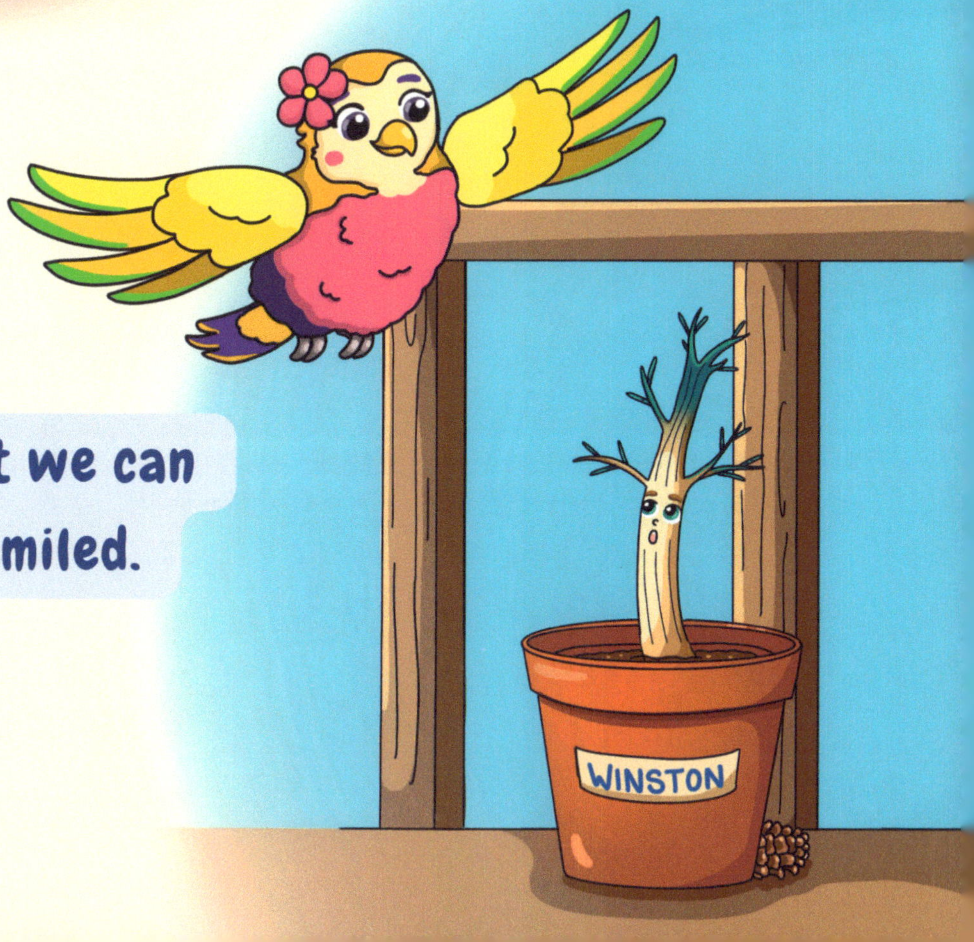

"Ooh no, Winston. But we can be friends." Quiche smiled.

"Am I a squirrel like you, Quark?" asked Winston.
"Ah, that's nuts, Winston." Quark giggled.
"Am I an owl like you, Alphie?" asked Winston.
"Whooo, you? It's best to be whooo you are, Winston," whispered Alphie.
WINSTON
WINSTON

Spring turned to summer, and Winston's toes became cramped in his pot.
WINSTON

"Winston, you are going to need more space to grow. Here is the perfect spot for you. The big trees will show you what to do," said Miss Higgz.

The Higgz family planted Winston beside the tall pine trees with great care. The creatures of the field watched. They were happy that Winston had found his place in the meadow.

Miss Higgz gave the soil around Winston a loving hug and some water.

Winston felt the cool water tickle his toes, the fresh breeze blow through his hair, and the warmth of the sun on his back. He stretched and wiggled his toes.

As the sun set, the Higgz family went home. Winston felt alone. He looked up at the big trees in wonder...

Could I be a tree? thought Winston. But I am sooo small.

Over the next months, Winston learned about the four seasons.
FALL

Each season came with a new challenge.
WINTER

From the dancing trees came a gentle whisper, 
SPRING
"Nevah... nevah... nevah evah give up."
SUMMER

With each new season, Winston grew stronger. 
HE MADE POLLEN FOR THE BEES.
And over the years, Winston grew taller and wiser. 
HE GREW PINE CONES WITH SEEDS TO FEED THE ANIMALS.

He even discovered some special gifts.

HE CLEANED THE AIR AND MADE SHADE FOR THE CREATURES.

HE BECAME A HOME FOR THE BIRDS.

Every creature of the field came to love Winston's strength and special gifts.

They even looked up to him. A new seedling grew up next to Winston and asked, "Winston, am I a tree like you?"

Winston smiled and said, "You sure are! Stick with me, and I'll show you what to do."

The wise owls shared a knowing glance as they looked out over the meadow. "Whoeee, Winston sure grew up!"

Shirley the snail looked up and giggled.
"That was fast!"

The End.

Higgzfield Friends

TO LEARN OUR NAMES THERE ARE LITTLE HINTS BELOW!

Quiche
Omega (Meg)
Alpha (Alphie)
SoTweet
Winston
Buzzy Bees
Muh

Winston's Special Gifts

He cleans the air and makes shade for the creatures.

He makes pollen for the bees.

He is a home for the birds.

He grows pine cones with seeds to feed the animals.

Winston creates new life: Winston Junior.

What are YOUR special gifts?

Just like Winston, you also have some special gifts. Sometimes, the things that seem different about us are what others like the most about us. Write or draw some of your special gifts in the boxes below!

For a free copy of this activity and other resources, visit www.higgzfield.com.

Other Higgzfield Tales

Upset feelings are okay, but they don't have to stay. Learn to let go of upset feelings using breath and movement with Quark and Boson!

Concepts:
Stress management
Emotional vocabulary
Friendship
Decision-making

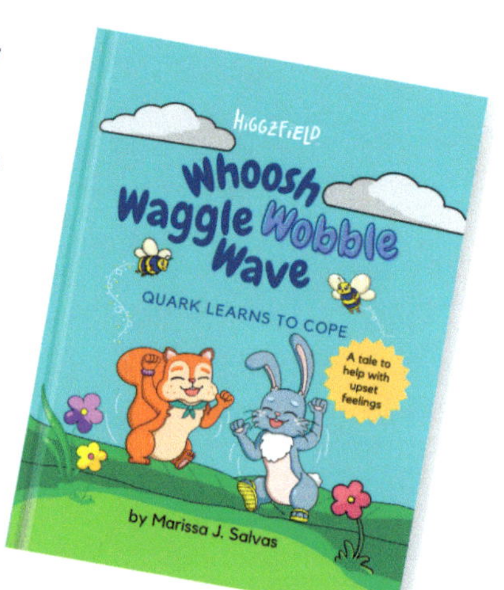

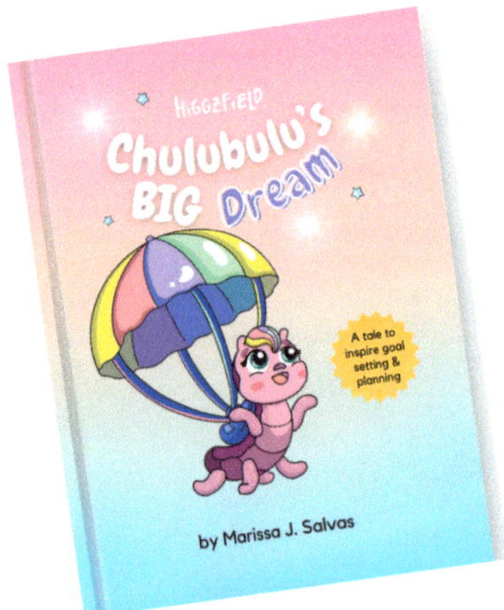

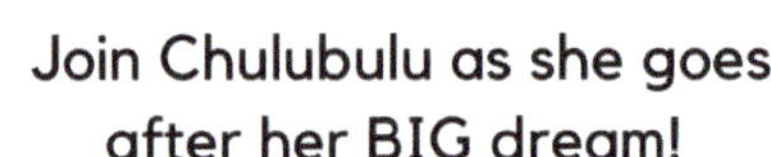

Join Chulubulu as she goes after her BIG dream!

Concepts:
Goal setting
Planning
Self-confidence
Friendship

To request a visit from the author email hello@higgzfield.com.

For free downloads and other insights,
visit www.higgzfield.com.

We love hearing from our readers!
Send your feedback or comments to
hello@higgzfield.com.

www.ingramcontent.com/pod-product-compliance
Lightning Source LLC
Chambersburg PA
CBHW042131030726
47599CB00002B/430